LOOK AGAIN!

THE *SECOND* ULTIMATE SPOT~THE~DIFFERENCE BOOK

Illustrated by APRIL WILSON

Nature notes by A.J.WOOD

A Puffin Pied Piper

For my family – A.W.

PUFFIN PIED PIPER BOOKS
Published by the Penguin Group
Penguin Books USA Inc., 375 Hudson Street, New York, New York, 10014, U.S.A.
Penguin Books Ltd, 27 Wrights Lane, London W8 5TZ, England
Penguin Books Australia Ltd, Ringwood, Victoria, Australia
Penguin Books Canada Ltd, 10 Alcorn Avenue, Toronto, Ontario, Canada M4V 3B2
Penguin Books (N.Z.) Ltd, 182–190 Wairau Road, Auckland 10, New Zealand
Penguin Books Ltd, Registered Offices: Harmondsworth, Middlesex, England

First published in hardcover in the United States 1992 by
Dial Books for Young Readers
A Division of Penguin Books USA Inc.

Devised and produced by The Templar Company plc, Surrey, Great Britain
Copyright © 1992 by The Templar Company plc
All rights reserved
Library of Congress Catalog Card Number: 91-31214
Printed in Italy

First Puffin Pied Piper Printing 1995
ISBN 0-14-055459-9
A Pied Piper Book is a registered trademark of
Dial Books for Young Readers,
a division of Penguin Books USA Inc.,
® TM 1,163,686 and ® TM 1,054,312.
1 3 5 7 9 10 8 6 4 2

LOOK AGAIN!
is also available in hardcover from
Dial Books for Young Readers.

*F*rom the ever-changing chameleon to the flower-like mantis, the bright stripes of the poisonous corn snake to the dramatic mating display of a jungle bird, the following pages illustrate a varied and wonderful use of color and form by some of the Earth's most fascinating creatures.

At first glance the pictures on facing pages may seem identical. But look again, and twelve vital differences will be revealed – a drab wood duck will become bright with breeding plumage, a Sumatran rabbit disappears amongst the undergrowth, or a fiddler crab reveals its colorful claw.

If you need help spotting the differences, turn to the back of the book. There, you'll also find a fascinating guide to the wonders of nature displayed in each pair of eye-challenging pictures.

HOW TO USE THIS BOOK

At the back of the book you will find a key to the contents of each pair of pictures. The twelve differences are highlighted in red. In some cases, one difference may involve several additions to the picture – more than one insect may have come to visit a flower, for example. In such cases, only one of these additions will be highlighted and these changes will only count as one out of the twelve to be discovered. All the various plant and animal species contained within the picture are also numbered in accordance with the guide that follows.

The floor of the European deciduous forest

The shallow waters of Australia's shore

The jungles of Central Africa

Wildlife of the polar regions

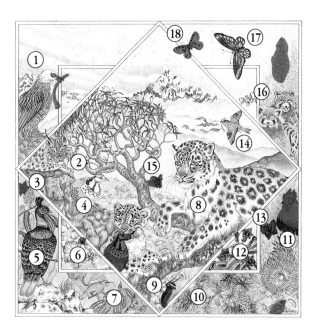

ON TOP OF THE WORLD
Flora and fauna of the Himalayas

Brilliant flowers and colorful birds brighten the summer slopes of these towering ranges that include Mt. Everest, the world's tallest peak. Many creatures have adapted to the harsh climate and remain high mountain dwellers all year. Others must descend to the lower slopes to survive the winter.

1. Lammergeier – The lammergeier or bearded vulture swoops high over the mountains indulging in a magnificent aerial courtship display. This shows off its tawny underside and black back that is used for camouflage when nesting on cliff ledges. It feeds on carrion and has learned the clever trick of flying into the air with large bones and dropping them onto rocks below so that they split and reveal their marrow.

2. Lynx – The lynx crouches stealthily among the rocks, hidden by its spotted coat as it waits for an unsuspecting bird or mammal to come within reach. It can kill with a single bite but its skill as a hunter has not saved it from near extinction. The lynx's shrinking forest habitat and its highly prized fur have both led to its decline.

3. Rhododendron – This native of the Himalayas brightens the mountainside with its colorful flowerheads, each made up of many purple cups. Cultivated forms are common, seen in a rainbow of colors throughout the world.

4. Snowcock – The snowcock blends in well with the background of its high-altitude home, working its way up the mountain slopes to search for roots, berries, and seeds. In the early morning it will fly downhill again to find water.

5. Impeyan pheasant – This thickset relative of the peafowl shines brilliantly against the snowy mountainside when the sun catches its iridescent blue-green plumage. The male raises his feather topknot when courting the female.

6. Himalayan poppy – The yellow center of this delicate flower is visited by pollinating insects. Its seeds can survive deep within the ground for hundreds of years.

7. Fire-tailed myzornis – The adaptable myzornis forages on foliage for its insect food and hovers like a hummingbird to drink nectar from flowers.

8. Snow leopard – The endangered snow leopard is a solitary creature, roaming a huge mountain territory alone unless it is a female out on a hunting trip with her young. Well adapted to its habitat, it spends summer above the tree line amid the snow, descending to the forests below for the duration of winter.

9. Tragopan – The male tragopan puffs out the blue feathers of his throat pouch to attract attention at the start of the mating season.

10. Ruby-cheeked sunbird – Flitting around flowers and foliage in a search for insects and nectar, these small birds bring a flash of color to the mountain scrub. They are clever builders, constructing a pear-shaped nest of plant fibers complete with entrance hole and overhanging porch.

11. Red junglefowl – The colorful junglefowl is the ancestor of the chicken, and scratches among the mountain scrub in much the same way as its farmyard counterpart, searching for grain, berries, and insect larvae. The cockerel displays his elaborate plumage, strutting in front of the duller, chestnut female. She will build a nest lined with leaves in a shallow scrape in the ground and raise a clutch of up to 6 well-camouflaged chicks.

12. Trumpet gentian – Like the rhododendron, the vivid blue gentian has been taken from its mountain home and cultivated as a garden plant. It attracts insects wherever it grows—whether brightening a mountain slope or a rock garden.

13. Himalayan jester – This brown and orange striped butterfly has markings that help to break up its outline, keeping it hidden from insect-eating birds.

14. Alpine accentor – This sparrowlike bird nests high up in the Tibetan mountains, at altitudes of over 17,000 feet. There is less competition for insect food at such heights since few species are adaptable enough to survive the extreme climate.

15. Himalayan tahr – The goatlike tahr is superbly adapted to its harsh habitat. Matching the color of the rocks, it can climb and leap about with ease.

16. Red panda – The lesser or red panda is a tree-dwelling, racoonlike creature, very different in size, shape, and color from its big, black and white relative. It spends the day curled up on a tree branch, covered by its camouflaged tail.

17. Delias butterfly – This insect carries a warning of its horrible taste in its yellow and black markings.

18. Apollo butterfly – There are many species of Apollo found in mountainous regions throughout the world. In the Himalayas this high-flying insect lives at altitudes of over 17,000 feet. Its red wing spots help confuse predators who may attack them rather than the body of the insect itself.

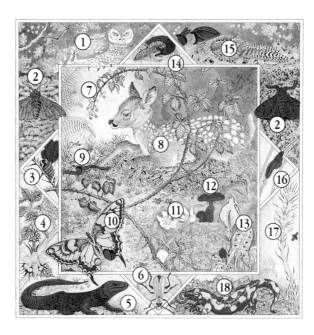

IN DAPPLED SUNLIGHT
The floor of the European deciduous forest

*I*n spring and early summer the forest floor abounds with life. Strolling among the trees, one will notice the bright flowers and insects, but many other creatures may remain hidden from the eye, camouflaged in their surroundings by their posture and color.

1. Little owl – One of the most common day-flying owls, the little owl is a bird of light woodland and open countryside. Protected by law, its barred plumage helps it blend into the woodland background as it sits motionless on post or branch.

2. Peppered moth – An example of evolution in progress, this moth can change its form to match its environment, adapting to new conditions to ensure survival. Before the Industrial Revolution, the dark or melanic form of the moth was extremely rare. It was normally white "peppered" with black specks, a color that stood out starkly against the soot-covered bark of the new generation of trees. The dark form, however, was well camouflaged under these changed circumstances and subsequently flourished.

3. Black hairstreak butterfly – One of the rarest forms of European hairstreak, the black variety has a curious chrysalis that uncannily resembles a bird dropping.

4. Yellow archangel – This relative of the mint commonly grows from the stumps of old trees. Its yellow, orchidlike flowers are streaked with rust-colored lines that direct insects to the center of the flower, thereby encouraging pollination.

5. Green and eyed lizards – Both these reptiles are camouflaged by their green skin. The eyed species can be identified by its bright blue spots.

6. Cardinal beetle – The vivid color of this insect warns predators that it is distasteful.

7. Bramble – The common bramble or blackberry is one of nature's great providers, forming dense thickets where a great variety of small mammals and birds find refuge. Its delicate flowers are visited by nectar-hunting insects, the grubs of flies, beetles, and moths (known as leaf miners) chew away the body of its leaves, and the juicy autumn berries are picked by hand and beak alike.

8. Roe deer fawn – Echoing the pattern of dappled sunlight on the forest floor, the brown and white spotted coat of the roe deer fawn hides its owner who waits, motionless, for its mother's return.

9. Slow worm – This legless lizard ranges in color from gray to shiny copper, matching the leaf-litter of the forest floor.

10. Swallowtail butterfly – Predators are often fooled into attacking the bright eye-spots on the hind wings of this glamorous butterfly, confused into thinking that they are the head of a different prey. The butterfly escapes with a damaged wing instead of a more serious injury.

11. Wood anemone – The flowers of this delicate plant open fully only on sunny days. Its white sepals attract insects that see at the ultraviolet end of the spectrum.

12. Fly agaric – This common fungi advertises its poisonous presence with a bright red cap dotted with white spots. These wash off during the autumn.

13. Wild arum – Known variously as cuckoo pint or lords and ladies, the wild arum is an exotic and unusual plant. Its color and smell attract insects that become trapped by hairs around the flowers' entrance. The insects remain imprisoned until the plant is pollinated. The hairs then wither and the prisoners are released to carry pollen to the next plant. The bright red berries are poisonous, as are all parts of the plant. Its tubers once provided the starch necessary to stiffen the ruff collars of the Elizabethans, but caused so much itching of the hands that it was replaced by starch from the potato, then newly-introduced from the Americas.

14. Great black slug – Camouflaged among the leaf litter, the great black slug comes out to feed in the cool of the night or on wet days. By doing so it avoids moisture loss from its slimy body.

15. Nightjar – In daytime this bird is almost invisible. It lies motionless on the ground, indistinguishable from the dead leaves that surround it. At twilight it takes to the air on soft-feathered wings, chasing insects that it catches in its huge mouth.

16. Tetragnatha spider – This wonderful grass mimic holds its legs out straight, mimicking a dead grass stem.

17. Common broomrape – The purple lines and spots of this plant act as honey-guides, directing insects to its nectaries. Its lack of green coloration is a clue to its parasitic nature. It need not make its own food through photosynthesis and therefore contains no green chlorophyll.

18. Fire salamander – The bright yellow markings of this amphibian warn that it is an irritant to the mouth of any predator.

SWAMP LAND
Wildlife of the Florida Everglades

*T*he hot, steamy swamps of Florida's Everglades are only a stone's throw from the bright lights of downtown Miami. Here a threatened wilderness survives—home of the alligator and mosquito and many other creatures.

1. Brown pelican – This bird, the smallest pelican, will dive into the water from as high as 50 feet to catch its fishy food. To protect it when it hits the water, it has a layer of air pockets under the skin of its breast. It is a sociable bird, nesting in great, noisy colonies among the mangrove trees.

2. Bullhead catfish – Grubbing in the mud of the river bottom, the catfish uses the sensory barbels around its mouth to help it search for its prey of insect larvae and mollusks.

3. Corn snake – The stripes of this corn snake make its outline hard to spot among the branches where it hunts its prey.

4. Limpkin – This well-camouflaged relative of the crane is now a protected species, having been hunted to near extinction earlier this century. It can be seen searching the swamp at dusk, probing the mud for water snails with its long beak.

5. Bromeliad – These epiphytic plants decorate mangrove trees throughout the Everglades. Their colorful bracts trap water to provide a mini aquatic habitat for insects and amphibians.

6. Lotus flower – An introduced species from Asia, the beautiful lotus rises up from the swamp water on its slender stem. Its color and smell attract insects for pollination.

7. Roseate spoonbill – This unusual bird sweeps the water with its oddly shaped bill, sifting for animal food—insect larvae, worms, water snails, tadpoles, and tiny fish. It also uses its bill as part of a courtship "dance," clapping the two halves together and raising its crest in display.

8. Custard apple – The plain exterior of the custard apple conceals its tasty yellow flesh that has a custardlike flavor.

9. Green ariole – A master of color change, this lizard can turn from green to brown in seconds, apparently disappearing before an intruder's very eyes. The male makes further use of color with his pink throat flap, fanning it out to attract the female during courtship.

10. Wood duck – This ornate duck is also known as the Carolina, tree, and summer duck —all of which provide clues to its lifestyle and habitat. Before the breeding season the male molts his "eclipse" plumage, which is like that of the female, to become a much more colorful creature, with his iridescent back and crest, white markings, and red beak.

11. Alligator – Floating lazily in the river or lying half submerged in the mud, the American alligator can easily be mistaken for a log—until it opens a beady eye or a hungry mouth. The female lays up to 50 eggs inside a mound of plant debris and remains close by until the eggs hatch about two months later. The young call out as a signal for their mother to open the nest and may remain with her for up to three years.

12. Eastern box turtle – The color and pattern of its shell helps hide the box turtle as it paddles through the swamp looking for slugs and worms. The shell markings differ widely among individuals.

13. Lubber grasshopper – Hopping through the saw grass or sitting motionless on the branch of a mangrove, this insect varies in color from green and yellow to pinkish brown. Like many other unobtrusive creatures, each individual is colored to blend in with the particular habitat where it spends its short life.

14. Tree snail – The shells of these snails decorate the mangrove branches like precious stones. Glistening after rain in a myriad of colors and patterns, they were prized by Native Americans who used them as a form of currency.

15. Ghost orchid – Stretching out over the muddy water, the delicate orchid lures insects to its nectar store by imitating an insect itself.

16. Gray tree frog – Clinging to the branches, this agile amphibian is well camouflaged. If disturbed it will flash the orange undersides of its legs to confuse predators.

17. Everglade kite – Also known as the snail kite, this bird of prey feeds only on water snails. It will hold one in its foot, waiting for the snail's head to emerge. Then the kite strikes with its specially elongated bill, shaking the snail free and allowing the empty shell to fall to the ground.

18. Red mangrove – The mangrove tree provides a home for many creatures of the swamp. Birds nest in its upper branches, fish and crabs shelter among its roots, and insects visit its small flowers searching for pollen and nectar. A tangled network of roots serves to both prop up the tree and offers a base for silt and materials brought in by the tide, building up the land. The long, embryonic root emerges from the seed while it is still attached to the parent plant, spearing the mud when it finally falls to grow into a new plant.

FANTASTIC FISH
The shallow waters of Australia's shore

*A*mong the myriad corals, glittering fish dart to and fro in search of food. Obscurity here is not provided by being colored drab brown or mottled green. Instead, the fish are brightly colored and patterned—helping each one to blend in with the rainbow reef that is their home.

1. Sea lemon – This aptly-named sea slug deters predators by emitting a strong acid from its mantle if disturbed.

2. Wrasse – The brilliantly colored wrasse vary in color and pattern with sex and age. They are highly territorial, only leaving their particular rocky patch to search for food. Many species will defend their homes by attempting to bite off the fins of any intruder.

3. Giant clam – This huge mollusk may weigh up to $1/4$ ton, but feeds only on minute food particles sifted from the water by its large gills. An undersea gardener of sorts, it provides a home for many single-celled algae in its colorful blue mantle. These algae live and photosynthesize within the clam's tissues, giving rise to green markings, and providing their giant host with both food and oxygen.

4. Feather star – This relative of the starfish waves its fronds through the water, wafting food particles toward its central mouth. Although it spends much of its life anchored to the rocks or reef by clawed stalks, it can cast off, swimming to a new spot with the help of its many arms.

5. Cleaner wrasse – The bright colors and dramatic stripes of this fish have a dual purpose. They advertise its presence to rivals and also to its customers—fish who, recognizing the cleaner's distinctive markings, allow it to swim around their bodies and in their mouths and gills, eating parasites as it goes.

6. Banded coral shrimp – Like the cleaner wrasse, this brightly colored shrimp removes parasites from fish that come to visit its home among the coral. It advertises its profession by waving its long antennae at possible customers, picking unwanted visitors from the fishes' scales with its hairy claws.

7. Beaked butterfly fish – The distinctive stripe running across this fish's head helps conceal its real eye—possibly its most vulnerable spot. The eyespot that develops near the adult's dorsal fin helps further confuse predators into thinking that its back is its head. It uses its beaklike snout to probe deep into crevices to find food.

8. Clownfish – This damselfish hides among the coral, concealed by its equally bright color. Unlike other reef fish, it is immune to the stinging tentacles of sea anemones and can find further refuge among their jellylike arms.

9. Choerodon fish – The bright colors of this fish change with age. Its protruding teeth are used to graze on the reef, scraping food from rocky surfaces.

10. Caesia fish – This curious reef fish changes color when it sleeps. It is red and green when asleep, blue-gray when awake.

11. Loggerhead turtle – The broad head of this marine turtle houses a powerful set of jaws—useful for crushing its hard-shelled prey of crabs and mollusks. It also eats the poisonous man-of-war jellyfish, attacking with eyes closed, and seemingly undeterred by the stinging tails of its prey.

12. Fiddler crab – Unlike the female, the male fiddler crab has one very large claw (the fiddle) and one small (the bow). The fiddle is useless for feeding or fighting and is only used for display.

13. Pied cormorant – The markings of this excellent fisherman help break up its outline as it swims underwater after prey.

14. Moorish idol – The striking markings and elaborate shape of the Moorish idol have long made it a favorite with artists, inspiring everything from fabric designs to wallpaper patterns, yet little is known of its lifestyle. The young look so different from the adults that they were once thought to be a separate species.

15. Cowrie – The spotted mantle of this mollusk can cover its shell entirely to hide it among the coral.

16. Clown triggerfish – To confuse predators this fish can turn to present a head-on view of its thin, diamond-shaped body—a total contrast to its large and spectacular profile.

17/18. Sea urchin and urchin shrimp – The body of the sea hedgehog or urchin is enclosed in a hard plated case, often covered in long, sharp spines. Urchin shrimps find refuge among the spines, matching the colors of their host as further defense against predators.

19. Tasseled wobbegong – Looking like a seaweed-covered rock, this carpet shark uses camouflage and cunning to catch its food. Unlike its fast-swimming relatives, it lies unseen on the seabed waiting to ambush its prey of fish and crustaceans.

CAMOUFLAGE AND COLOR
The jungles of Central Africa

*F*rom the shaded floor to the top of the forest canopy, every level of the African rain forest is home to a multitude of creatures. Many, such as the monkeys, rarely descend to the ground, spending their whole lives leaping among the branches.

1. African linsang – Its spotted coat and banded tail help hide this civet as it climbs through the trees. It spends the day asleep in a nest of vegetation and emerges at night to hunt insects and young birds.

2. Diana monkey – This elegant monkey uses its color and markings to proclaim its identity in the forest. Chiefly eating fruit, leaves, and buds, it will also steal birds' eggs and young.

3/4. Amauris and papilio butterflies – Just as the pericopine moth mimics the postman butterfly for protection, the harmless papilio mimics several distasteful butterflies, including the brown and white amauris shown here. The amauris is an example of Mullerian mimicry—in which several different species look similar and are all well-protected against predators. This phenomenon is named after the German explorer Fritz Müller who first observed it.

5. Pseudocreobotra mantis – This exotic insect has dramatic "eyes" on its wings. When startled, it will open them in threat display, revealing a menacing "face." Like some other mantids, the female of this

species will eat the male—after or even during mating! Before laying her eggs, she secretes a gummy liquid, stirring it into a frothy mass. It will harden to form a series of chambers into which the eggs are laid.

6. Mandrill – The colorful mandrill has a striking area of bare skin on its snout, vividly grooved and striped in red and blue. Most monkeys have excellent eyesight and use color to the full—to proclaim their sex or species, or in threat or mating display.

7. Aletis moth – The bright orange wings warn of this moth's horrible taste. Males and females link together as they fly through the forest, mating in midair.

8. Water chevrotain – The white stripes and spots of this mouse deer—so called because of its diminutive size and mouselike head—help to hide its outline among the deep undergrowth. It always lives near freshwater and is adept at catching fish, crabs, and small mammals, although it normally forages for leaves and fruit.

9. Bush pig – This bristly creature, also known as the red river hog, snuffles on the forest floor, rooting for food with its long snout. The black and white markings on its

face help identification within the group. This may consist of up to a dozen individuals, led by an old boar.

10. Rhampholeon marshalli – Not content with the ability to change color, this chameleon has a flattened body and humped back to aid its disguise as a leaf. It will grasp a branch and sway from side to side as though blown by the wind.

11. Hingeback tortoise – This tortoise spends most of its life hiding, half buried under the debris of the forest floor. It has hinged back plates on its shell that fold down, covering its rear when attacked.

12. White-cheeked mangabey – This noisy monkey, with its untidy tufts of hair, leaps through the trees—jumping as much as 20 feet from branch to branch.

13. Bongo – The timid bongo rests by day, deep under the cover of the undergrowth where its striped coat helps hide it from view.

14. Goliath beetle – The aptly named goliath beetle has the largest body of any insect, measuring nearly 4 inches. It is 8 million times heavier than the world's smallest beetle. The female lacks the horns of the male.

15. Red colobus – This jungle acrobat was

once thought to be a messenger of the gods, due to its habit of climbing to the tops of high trees at sunrise and sitting as if in prayer.

16. Hyperolius frog – This brightly striped frog fools predators by moving if approached. When it does, the changing pattern of its stripes makes its outline disappear.

17. Superb sunbird – The female of this species hardly deserves her name with her drab olive-green plumage. But it helps to hide her as she sits on her untidy nest of leaves and lichen. By contrast, the male is a multi-colored vision of metallic green, purple, and deep red.

18. Red-billed fire finch – One of the most common African birds, this member of the waxbill family is often seen in towns and villages, searching for grass and other seeds. Many waxbill nestlings have striking patterns on the inside of their mouths that stimulate the adults to feed them.

19. Red-crested turaco – The bright red and green plumage of this turaco may look vivid as it basks in the African sun. But sitting on a branch deep in the forest it is much more difficult to spot. It raises its crest in alarm to attract attention.

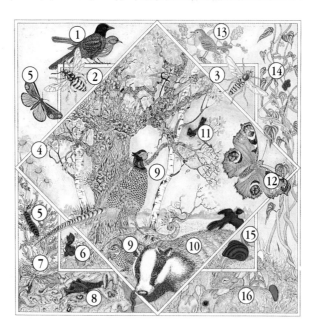

WOODLAND EDGE
Wildlife of field and forest

Temperate deciduous forests once covered most of Europe in a virtually unbroken green blanket. As civilization has encroached, many forest animals have adapted to living in fields and hedgerows, but still rely on the shrinking woodlands for food and shelter.

1. Blackbird – The flutelike song of the blackbird echoes through woods and across fields and gardens. Males will indulge in display fights in the spring, their bills turning bright orange as an indication of their breeding condition. The mottled brown female lays up to 5 blue-green eggs in a neat cup of dry grass and will continue to feed her young after they have left the nest.

2/3. Common wasp and hoverfly – The hoverfly comes in many different guises, imitating the color pattern of more dangerous bees and wasps as a crafty form of defense. A closer inspection shows that the hoverfly has a smoother body, a quite un-wasplike manner of flight, hovering with fast-beating wings over the flowers on which it feeds, and no sting in its tail. The wasp warns of its nasty sting with dramatic yellow and black stripes—a warning signal that is used by many other animal species, from snakes to caterpillars.

4. Ragwort – The yellow heads of the ragwort are common on roadsides, in fields, and other grassy places throughout Europe, and plains throughout the United States. They contain a poison that can be fatal to horses and cattle if eaten, but is beneficial to the cinnabar caterpillar who absorbs it to become poisonous itself.

5. Cinnabar moth – One of the few day-flying moths, the cinnabar's bright colors warn that it contains poison, passed on from the food plant it ate as a caterpillar. The larvae also sport warning colors with their contrasting stripes of yellow and black. Great colonies of them often smother ragwort stems in the summer. They spend the winter as dull brown chrysalises.

6. Speedwell – The blue flowers of this plant dot the woodland floor in early summer. A closer inspection will reveal a set of tiny lines on the petals, directing insects to its nectaries.

7. Green oak moth – The larva of this moth lives on oak leaves, rolling them around itself for protection. The delicate green adult is almost impossible to spot among the foliage —its daytime resting place.

8. Oak bushcricket – Camouflaged among leaves, the only clue to the bushcricket's presence may be the sound of its "song" made by the bases of its front wings being rubbed together.

9. Pheasant – The pheasant was introduced to Europe from Asia over seven centuries ago and hybrids and relatives are also found in the United States. The male is a decorative sight with his coppery plumage, red wattles, and white collar, driving away rivals with loud calls and an aggressive display. The hen and her young are well-camouflaged with their speckled brown plumage. If they are disturbed, the female has another trick of defense. She will feign injury, trailing a wing and drawing the intruder away from the nest before disappearing into the undergrowth again.

10. Badger – This elusive creature emerges from its home or sett as darkness falls, out on a nocturnal hunt for its favorite food: earthworms. The markings on its head are thought to help recognition between individuals but may also serve to warn other animals to keep away from its powerful bite.

11. Holly blue butterfly – A fierce defender of its territory, this insect will drive away others of its species with an energetic aerial display. Other pale blue objects that appear on its "patch" often get the same treatment.

12. Peacock butterfly – This insect looks like a dead leaf with its raggedy wings closed. But they can be used successfully to startle an enemy, opening to reveal four beautifully marked "eyes," colored like those on a peacock's tail.

13. Robin – The red-breasted robin uses its colorful front to advertise its presence, loudly singing and threatening any red object that enters its territory. It has been known to attack even inanimate red objects, such as balls of wool, with gusto.

14. Black bryony – This hedgerow climber has bright red berries in the autumn, warning of their poisonous content.

15. Brown-lipped snail – The color and banding of these snails varies widely. Yellow, green, and a multitude of different browns are found, each blending in with the color of its particular background.

16. Rabbit – Four young rabbits lie sleeping in their burrow, soon to embark on life above ground. At the first sign of danger, rabbits will thump the ground loudly before hopping to safety. The flashing white underside of their "cottontails" acts as a further warning to take cover.

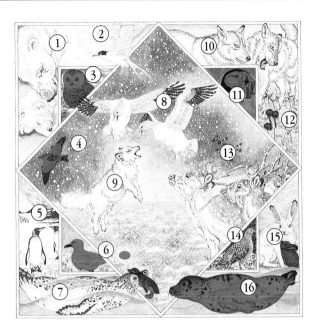

SNOWDRIFTS AND ICEBERGS
Wildlife of the polar regions

*T*he land of the high polar regions, perhaps the Earth's last true wilderness, is one where the wildlife changes with the seasons. Many of those that live in this frigid climate are transformed in the winter months into creatures that are as white as the ice and snow that surround them.

1. Polar bear – The unmistakable polar bear roams the ice floes of the Arctic, its creamy white coat merging with the snowy landscape. Its fur is useful in other ways—each white hair absorbing infrared heat from the sun like a tiny, transparent optical fiber.

2. Arctic tern – Flying 11,000 miles from one end of the globe to the other, the Arctic tern is a record-breaker of the bird world. It nests in the high Arctic, where its mottled eggs look like pebbles on the stony ground, and winters in far away Antarctica—making the 22,000 mile round-trip every year.

3. Snowy owl – The snowy white male and the darkly barred female fly silently over the Arctic tundra, searching for their prey of hares and small rodents as well as birds such as ducks and gulls. Unusually, these owls hunt by day, their plumage helping to conceal them from their hapless victims. The female's darker color helps her to blend in with the rock-strewn tundra where she makes her nest.

4. Snow bunting – In winter the male snow bunting has white plumage mottled with rusty brown. In the summer he flies farther north to breed, molting to become almost pure white.

5. King penguin – Most at home in the water, the penguin's dark back and pale front make it hard to spot—blending with the dark depths of the Antarctic seas when seen from above or merging with the pale light filtering down through the surface waters when viewed from below.

6. Ivory gull – The only pure white gull, the bill of both sexes carries an orange spot. The darker young automatically peck this on hatching, thereby stimulating the adults to regurgitate food for them.

7. Leopard seal – With its slender, torpedo-shaped body the leopard seal glides effortlessly through the cold Southern Ocean, a part of the teeming life that make these waters as rich in life-forms as any in the world. Its spotted coat conceals it in the watery depths. It catches penguins both on and off the ice to supplement its diet of squid, fish, and crustaceans.

8. Snow goose – The snow goose lays its eggs in a scrape on the ground, relying on camouflage to conceal it from predators.

Should the camouflage fail, the parent birds will mob any attacker in an effort to drive it away from their helpless young.

9. Arctic fox – Like many other animals of the Arctic, the fox changes color to match the seasons—gray-brown in summer to match the tundra, pure white in winter for camouflage against the snow.

10. Arctic wolf – A variation of the gray wolf, the Arctic race varies in color according to its habitat. In the most northern parts of their range these intelligent and much-maligned creatures have white coats all year round.

11. Puffin – The comical puffin puts its large bill to good use, filling it with many fish that it carries back to its nest at one time. After the breeding season, the striped bill becomes gradually dull, the bird loses its red eye patch, and its white head feathers turn to gray.

12. Arctic poppy – Yellow poppies carpet the tundra to mark the coming of the Arctic spring. Along with other flowers, they bring a surge of color to this seemingly barren landscape. The poppies' stems are insulated with hairs against the cold, and their color attracts insects for pollination.

13. Caribou – The caribou or reindeer was once divided into several species, varying in color from black through brown and gray, to almost white. It is now thought that they are all variations of one species, adapting their coats to blend in with their different backgrounds. Unlike other deer, both males and females carry antlers. They feed on the plants of the tundra, scraping away the winter snow with their hooves to feed on the lichens below.

14. Ptarmigan – An expert at color change, the ptarmigan molts three times a year. In spring it is a mottled brown to match the rocks among which it breeds. In autumn it is gray to match the tundra where it feeds, and in winter it's as white as snow.

15. Arctic hare – Also known as the snowshoe hare, this animal changes from brown to white in winter too. Its ears are smaller than those of ordinary hares to reduce heat loss through the thin skin. The young are gray when born.

16. Harp seal – The harp seal pup is mainly white at birth, camouflaged against the pack ice on which it lives. It develops the marked coat of the adult and starts independent life after about four weeks.

STILL WATER SPRING
European freshwater wildlife

*T*he arrival of spring heralds a burst of color at the water's edge—many creatures are resplendent in bright breeding colors, spring flowers advertise their presence to pollinators with showy petals—and land, sky, and water teem with life after the silence of winter.

1. Aeshna dragonfly – One of the fastest of all insects, the dragonfly provides a familiar flash of color as it darts around and above the water. The brilliant metallic colors of the adults are used for territorial display and any intruder is rigorously driven away.

2. Marsh marigold – Also known as the kingcup, this majestic marsh plant has bright yellow petals, complete with "honey-guide" lines that attract insects to the flower's pollen center.

3. Mallard – The ancestors of most domesticated ducks, the duck and drake mallard are hard to distinguish for part of the year. But in the breeding season the drake is transformed by color. With his glossy green head, white collar, and elaborate courtship display, he hopes to find a mate. As many as 12 ducklings may be raised by the mottled brown female.

4. Water crowfoot – To insects that see at the ultraviolet end of the spectrum, the water crowfoot appears as a pale flower with a vivid blue center, attracting them to its pollen and nectar store.

5. Great crested newt – Emerging from his winter hibernation on land, the male of this species returns to water in the spring, donning a new appearance to attract a mate. His belly becomes a fiery orange and the spotted crest along his back becomes more pronounced. With luck he will find a female, fertilizing her eggs before they are laid on the leaves of water plants.

6. Toad spawn – Unlike the eggs (spawn) of other amphibians such as frogs and newts, toad spawn is laid in distinctive long strings.

7. Tench – The strong-bodied tench has smooth, green skin covered with tiny scales. This gives it a matt appearance that helps camouflage it among the murky water.

8. Water vole – Gnawing vegetation at the pond edge, the water vole is alert to danger. At the slightest sight or sound of an intruder, it will dive into the water, leaving only a loud "plop" and a stream of bubbles as a clue to its existence.

9. Common frog – The common frog is, unfortunately, less common than it used to be—threatened by pollution and destruction of its habitat. Its smooth, mottled skin varies in color with its background—ranging from green and gray to brown, yellow, and even pink. Spawn is laid in a mass in still water in the Spring. The tadpoles develop legs and reabsorb their tails before taking to life on land.

10. Grass snake – Well camouflaged in its grassy environment, this shy reptile cannot rely on a poisonous bite for protection since it does not possess one. Instead it will hiss loudly, dart its head rapidly back and forth, and emit a foul-smelling liquid in an effort to deter any attacker. If this fails, it may even feign death, lying belly-up on the ground.

11. Flatworm – Looking like a blob of brown jelly, the flatworm crawls over the detritus of the pond bed. Each individual contains both male and female organs, and if cut in half, can regenerate into two new worms.

12. China mark moth – The unusual larva of this night-flying moth spends its life underwater, hiding itself among the debris by making a case of plant matter in which to live. As an adult it relies on its beautifully marked wings to conceal it from hungry birds.

13. Three-spined stickleback – Another colorful suitor, the male stickleback develops a bright red underside in the spring breeding season. This is used to repel rivals and attract the silvery gray female to a nest of plant matter built by the male fish in the center of his territory.

14. Pitcher plant – This carnivorous plant lures unsuspecting insects into its death trap using its smell and color. They fall into the well of liquid contained within its urn-shaped leaves where they gradually dissolve and are absorbed into the plant tissue.

15. Eyed hawk moth – This beautifully marked moth looks like a dead willow leaf when hiding in the daytime. But if disturbed, it will startle a predator by exposing the false "eyes" on its hind wings, hence its common name. The green caterpillar has a distinctive "horn" on the end of its body and feeds on the leaves of willow trees.

16. Red underwing – Invisible when resting on the bark of a tree, this moth will open its wings to fly away if disturbed, revealing an unexpected flash of color. The surprise appearance of its red hind wings may confuse a would-be predator long enough to allow the moth its escape.

17. Kingfisher – This expert fisherman dives for its food, speeding through the air like a shining blue bullet with beautiful colors that warn predators of its distasteful flesh.

AROUND THE WATERHOLE
Wildlife of the desert and scrub

*I*n the shimmering heat of the desert the waterhole provides a gathering place for a great variety of creatures. The water may not last for long. Unless it is fed by an underground spring, the oasis will soon dry up, reappearing again after the heavy rains of spring.

1. Carmine bee-eater – Great flocks of these colorful birds congregate at waterholes, making them one of the most spectacular species in the Old World. Their bright colors play an important role in defense of the nest burrows, dug with bill and feet in sandy riverbanks and sometimes extending for 8 feet into the soft soil.

2. Fennec fox – As sandy in color as its desert background, the fennec is the smallest of foxes. Its large ears are a clue to its excellent hearing—essential for the detection of food, enemies, and mates. They also assist in temperature control, giving out excess heat like two living radiators.

3. Mesembryanthemum – Common as a cultivated garden plant, these many-petaled flowers bring color to the desert and attract insects with their bright display.

4. Impala – The impala herd uses the distinctive markings of each individual to confuse any would-be predator. If disturbed, the whole herd will leap straight into the air in all directions, jumping to and fro in a jumbled mass of brown, black, and white. The countershading of their handsome coat—dark back, paler belly—helps to counteract the shadow effect of light falling from above, flattening their image so that it merges more easily with the background. This type of shading is seen in almost all wild animals.

5. Giraffe – The extraordinary giraffe is the tallest animal in the world. Its patterned coat assists in camouflaging but has also led to the giraffe's decline in some parts of Africa, hunted to near extinction for its hide. A number of races of giraffe exist within one species, varying in their color from chestnut to almost black.

6. Eronia butterfly – The pattern of dark veins and blotches on its wings serves to hide this insect against its background. The underside of the wings is more heavily patterned.

7. Cheetah – Once found from India to Africa's southernmost tip, this big cat is now rare or extinct in most parts of its former range. The fastest land animal, it can reach a speed of 70 mph but only over short distances. Its normal hunting tactic is to stalk its prey, hiding among long grasses, creeping closer and closer until it breaks into the final rapid chase.

8. Desert grasshopper – When disturbed, this Australian insect will open its wings to reveal a brightly striped abdomen. This usually confuses its enemies for long enough to allow it to hop or fly away.

9. Caracal – The sandy-colored caracal, also known as the Persian lynx, uses its black-tufted ears for signaling. This beautiful killer hunts prey from antelopes and monkeys, to reptiles and small birds.

10. Living stone plants – An apparent pile of pebbles, so convincing in their shape and pattern, is transformed by spring rain into a group of colorful plants.

11. Cape springhare – This African rodent has been described variously as a mouse, a squirrel, and a porcupine. It now occupies a family all its own as a jumping hare, *spring haas* in Afrikaans. Leaping 10 feet in one bound, this kangaroo-like creature will jump suddenly in a different direction to escape its attackers, using its bushy tail as a counterbalance.

12. Meerkat – This member of the mongoose family lives in family units, in groups of 30 or more individuals. A constant watch is kept for danger, the sentries sitting bolt upright to survey the surrounding bush. Their markings help with colony communication and may help to deceive their main enemies—birds of prey.

13. Yellow-throated sand grouse – This relative of the pigeon lives in sandy deserts and rocky outcrops throughout the dry parts of Africa. Its color varies from reddish brown to gray, depending on its particular habitat and this, together with its marked plumage, makes it hard to spot. The sand grouse is said to sometimes lay its eggs in the footprints of animals, where they are difficult to find among the sand. Parent birds are also reputed to carry water back to their nesting young, fluffing up their feathers in the waterhole to trap precious droplets in their dense underdown.

14. Blue-tongued skink – This desert-dwelling Australian reptile will stick out its vivid purplish-blue tongue as a colorful form of defense.

15. Saw-scaled adder – This viper hides by day among rocks and tree trunks, or half covered by the desert sand. If disturbed, it rubs the scales on its sides together to make a threatening sound.

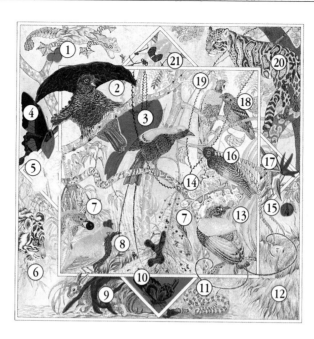

PARADISE LOST?
In the jungles of Indonesia and New Guinea

Like Earth's other jungles, those of Indonesia and New Guinea are rich in fantastic life forms. Some of the world's most beautiful creatures live here, though they must battle for survival as the spread of civilization goes on.

1. Kuhl's gecko – The strange flaps of skin along the sides and between the toes of this so-called "flying" gecko have a two-fold purpose. They are used to form a sort of parachute when the gecko launches itself through the air. More importantly, they are pressed down against the bark when it flattens itself against a branch in hiding, removing any shadows that might otherwise reveal its presence. The gecko's sticky eggs are laid on a tree branch where they remain, stuck fast for some 6 months until the young finally hatch.

2. Superb bird of paradise – Perhaps the most visually spectacular of all bird families, the birds of paradise are found only in the rain forests of this small corner of the Earth. As with all species, the male courts the female with a stunning display, puffing out his turquoise breast shield and neck crest in a huge fan of color.

3. Greater bird of paradise – The males of this species gather to display in the same tree, attracting as many mates as they can by raising the feathery white plumes on their backs and dancing along the branches.

4/5. Papilio butterfly and orchid

mantis – The flowerlike mantis uses its pretty disguise to fool insect-eating birds and also to catch insect meals of its own. Unsuspecting butterflies are lured between the petallike extensions on its limbs in a search for nectar. Too late they find themselves grasped by the "flower's" forelegs.

6. Tiger – The magnificent tiger once roamed through forests from Siberia to Java. Sadly, the twin threats of indiscriminate hunting and the destruction of its natural habitat have taken their toll. Many races are rare or thought to be extinct.

7. McGregor's bowerbird – Perhaps the greatest architects of the bird world, the male bowerbirds attract their mates by building elaborate "pavilions" of twigs and decorating them with color. McGregor's, or the gardener, bowerbird builds a pole of twigs surrounded by a moss garden, littering it with flowers, berries, pebbles, insects, and even bottle tops. Like all members of this bird family, the female will then build a functional nest in which to hatch her eggs.

8. Sickle-crested bird of paradise – The brilliant orange male of this species raises his head feathers when courting a mate.

9. Sumatran rabbit – This extremely rare creature is the only rabbit with a striped coat, helping it to mingle with the undergrowth.

10. Swallowtail butterfly – Like many butterflies, this species will bend its wings to lose its shadow when alighting in a sunny spot.

11. Eastern brownsnake – This venomous reptile moves swiftly over the forest floor, searching for frogs and small mammals.

12. Orangutan – The name of this strange ape means "man of the woods" in Malay. It is the second-largest primate after the gorilla and spends most of its life in the trees. Its reddish-brown coat looks like stringy bark or dead leaves as it rests in its nest of twigs high above the jungle floor.

13. Magnificent bird of paradise – This bird makes up for his small size with a colorful costume and breathtaking display. Over a cleared patch of forest, he sits on a branch, spreading his mantle and puffing out his chest so that it appears to throb.

14. Vanda orchid – Like many orchids, this species is an insect mimic. Male insects will fly to its flowers, fooled into believing that they have found a mate, and pollinate the plant in the process.

15. Nutmeg – The yellow, fleshy fruit of this fragrant evergreen splits when ripe to reveal the bright red covering of its seed. It is widely cultivated for both the covering (mace) and the seed itself (nutmeg). Both are used as spices.

16. King of Saxony's bird of paradise – Bouncing up and down on a branch, hissing and puffing up his feathers, the male of this species calls to his mate. He will wave his wirelike head plumes in front of her before mating, but takes no part in making a nest or rearing the young.

17. Syzygium – The new red growth of this bush warns of its poisonous content.

18. Green broadbill – The plumage of this bird hides it in the dense, green forest where it builds a pear-shaped nest.

19. Rainbow lorikeet – Unlike many other creatures of the forest, this small parrot is seen living close to man in plantations, parks, and gardens.

20. Clouded leopard – The powerful body of this elusive hunter is covered with a beautifully-patterned coat, concealing its shape as it moves through the shadows.

21. Leaf beetle – As its name reveals, this insect feeds on leaves and flowers.

LIGHTING UP THE DARKNESS
Luminous life of the deep ocean

*F*ar out at sea, birds wheel in the sky above the vast blue ocean. The surface waters are filled with sunlight, but dive deeper and one enters a world of darkness. Here, some creatures make their own light, using chemicals or bacteria trapped in special organs underneath their scales.

1. Red-tailed tropic bird – This bird's white plumage becomes rosy in the breeding season, when it will build a nest on a cliff ledge.

2. Box fish – The startling colors of the box fish warn of its defense speciality. When attacked, it squirts poison into the water—enough to deter many predators.

3. Comb jelly – No one knows exactly how the comb jellies give off their luminous light, flashing on and off as they swim in shoals through the water.

4. Deep-sea dragonfish – With a mouth full of teeth ready to bite, the dragonfish swims through the darkness. Red spots and white lines glow on its body and it trails a luminous "lure"—a greatly elongated piece of skin that looks like a worm to a hungry victim.

5. Viper fish – Deep-sea fish are often equipped with lures and lights. This one uses the elongated ray of its dorsal fin as a lure, moving it forward to dangle in front of a fearsome mouth, equipped with the long, fanglike teeth that have earned it its name. The viper's main prey is the lantern fish.

6. Linophryne arborifera – This deep-sea angler has what looks like a piece of seaweed hanging from its chin and a luminous lure growing out from its nose. When the lure is touched, the mouth opens immediately and consumes its prey.

7. Sea otter – This mammal dives to the seabed to collect its food of crabs, clams, sea urchins, mussels, and other mollusks, picking up a stone at the the same time. Then it floats on its back with the stone on its chest and cracks open its hard-shelled catch by banging it against the stone.

8. Moray eel – The boldly patterned moray hides in rock crevices waiting to ambush its unsuspecting prey. It is a vicious hunter and can deliver a nasty bite if startled.

9. Goosefish – An elongated spine tipped with a flap of skin is waved in front of this fish's head as it lies perfectly camouflaged on the seabed, waiting for a victim to mistake the lure for a tasty morsel. It then opens its huge mouth when a meal is in sight, sucking the unfortunate fish to its death.

10. Marine iguana – The only marine lizard, this iguana is most at home in the water, swimming and diving for its meals of seaweed. The males are highly territorial, developing a green crest and red patches to signal defense of their breeding grounds.

11. Squid – The jet-propelled squid has luminescent organs for communication. It can change its appearance to match its background or literally ripple with color—either when mating or catching prey. Squid are some of the fastest animals in the sea. Some small species can even propel themselves out of the water, flying through the air over distances of 150 feet.

12. Pacific fang tooth fish – This hatchet fish has light-producing organs on its belly that are arranged in a particular pattern. This helps the various species to recognize one another in the dark oceans.

13. Lantern fish – Here the light-producing organs illuminate the surrounding water like spotlights, assisting this fish in its search for plankton. They also help males and females recognize one another.

14. Portuguese man-of-war – The man-of-war is not a single animal but a colony of polyps. One type forms a purple, translucent float—a crested bag of gas that catches the wind like a sail to carry the colony across the waves. The others form chains that hang down in the water and take care of feeding and reproduction. Perhaps most impressive are the long, stinging tentacles that drift behind this jellyfish for up to 50 feet. They are armed with a sting as powerful as a cobra's venom and paralyze any fish that swim into them.

15. Sargassum fish – This curious frog fish is covered with bumps and flaps of skin that help it blend in with the sargassum weed in which it lives. Color varies from one fish to another but always matches each individual's seaweed patch. If sought out by a predator, it will fill itself up with water, becoming a huge ball too big for its attacker to swallow.

16. Wandering albatross – With a 10-foot wingspan, this is the longest-winged bird in the world. It glides on the strong ocean winds, landing only to breed. Albatrosses mate for life, returning to the same breeding spot every other year. There, they indulge in a spectacular courtship display, dancing with bills touching and wings outstretched. They lay a single egg in a cup-shaped nest.